TREES AND SHRUBS

"Eyes and No Eyes" Series

by Arabella B. Buckley

- I. Wild Life in Woods and Fields
- II. By Pond and River
- III. Plant Life in Field and Garden
- IV. Birds of the Air
- V. Trees and Shrubs
- VI. Insect Life

by R. Cadwallader Smith

- VII. On the Seashore
- VIII. Within the Deep
- IX. Riverside Rambles
- X. Highways and Hedgerows
- XI. Nature's Nurseries
- XII. O'er Moor and Fen

"EYES AND NO EYES" SERIES   BOOK V

TREES AND SHRUBS

BY

ARABELLA B. BUCKLEY

YESTERDAY'S CLASSICS
CHAPEL HILL, NORTH CAROLINA

Cover and arrangement © 2008 Yesterday's Classics, LLC.

This edition, first published in 2008 by Yesterday's Classics, an imprint of Yesterday's Classics, LLC, is an unabridged republication of the text originally published by Cassell and Company, Ltd. in 1901. For the complete listing of the books that are published by Yesterday's Classics, please visit www.yesterdaysclassics.com. Yesterday's Classics is the publishing arm of the Baldwin Online Children's Literature Project which presents the complete text of hundreds of classic books for children at www.mainlesson.com.

ISBN-10: 1-59915-275-4

ISBN-13: 978-1-59915-275-2

Yesterday's Classics, LLC
PO Box 3418
Chapel Hill, NC 27515

CONTENTS

I. The Value of Trees 1

II. How a Tree Starts 5

III. How a Tree Grows—
The Horse-Chestnut 11

IV. Trees with Catkin Flowers 17

V. The British Oak 24

VI. Guests of the Oak 30

VII. The Beech and the Sweet
Chestnut 37

VIII. Trees Which Bear Cones 42

IX. Hedgerow Shrubs and Trees 49

X. Garden Shrubs in Bloom 55

XI. The Ash and the Elm 61

XII. In the Park 67

XIII. Leaves—Their Shape and
Position 73

CHAPTER I
THE VALUE OF TREES

I wonder if you have ever stopped to think how useful trees are in the world. We saw in Book III. that plants make the air pure for us to breathe. Trees, with their hundreds of leaves, do a large part of this work, and they do a great deal besides.

Let us imagine a little tree growing up in the wood, or in the field. It may perhaps be eaten away by rabbits or squirrels before it is a year old. If so, it has been useful as food. But if it grows up, it begins even the first year to drop some leaves in the autumn, and these help to make leaf-mould, and so give food for other plants.

So it goes on each year, making leaves, purifying the air, and producing leaf-mould. But very soon insects begin to make their home in the young sapling, for every kind of tree has some insects living on it. A moth comes and lays her eggs under the leaves, and the caterpillars feed on them when they are hatched. A beetle comes and lays her eggs in the bark, and the grub feeds there, till it turns into a beetle, or till the woodpecker or the nuthatch find and eat it.

In this way every tree is quite a little colony of living creatures. Then the birds come and sleep in its boughs at night and build their nests there in the spring. If the trees are elms the rooks often choose them for their rookery. If they are firs in a wood the woodpigeon will sleep there, or pheasants and hawks perch on their branches, while the thrush and the blackbird spend the night in laurels, or hollies and other evergreen trees.

When the tree has grown big it bears flowers and fruits. These fruits, or the seeds in them, serve as food for many creatures. The birds feed on the berries, the nuts, and the acorns. The squirrel makes its home in the beech-trees, and eats all kinds of nuts it can find. The field-mouse, hedgehog, and pig make good meals off the beech-nuts and acorns on the ground, while we eat the fruit of the sweet chestnut and the walnut tree, the apples, pears and cherries from the orchard.

How useful the trees are to man! They help to keep the ground moist and fresh. There is always more rain in a country where there are trees, and the ground would grow parched and dry, if it were not for their pleasant shade. How the cattle gather under them, when the sun is bright, and stand chewing the cud so peacefully out of the glare and heat! And how glad you are on your way to school, if you can walk through a shady lane instead of along the high road. Then they

THE VALUE OF TREES

are so beautiful in the spring; when the fresh green leaves burst out they make us glad to think that every year tree-life begins again.

On the other hand, some trees are so old, several hundreds of years, that they remind us of times long gone by, and make us love our country when we think what a long history those trees could tell.

But even trees must die at last, and, if they are to be of use to us we must cut them down before they decay. Then, after the tree is dead, how useful it is!

Let us just go through one day of your life, and see how much of a tree you use. You get up in the morning, and the first thing to be done is to light a fire with wood. You sit on a chair: that is made of wood. You open the door that is of wood too. You take up your umbrella when you start for school: the handle was once the bough of a tree. You go upstairs to fetch your bag: the stairs are made out of planks. You set off on your way, and have to cross a brook: the bridge is made of wood. You are careful to shut the gate of the field: that, too, is made of a tree, and so is the paling round the school.

You take your place in class. Your feet rest on deal planks which come from the fir-tree. You sit on a wooden bench. Your slate has a wooden frame. Your pen has a wooden handle. The teacher puts up a wooden easel and a wooden blackboard upon it. She opens the ink-bottle to fill the inkstands, and the cork of the bottle

TREES AND SHRUBS

comes from the bark of a tree, while the ink itself is made with acid which comes from a gall made by an insect on an oak-tree.

Dinner-time comes. Surely, now, you will not want any wood. You fetch your basket with your dinner in it. That may be made of wood-chips or willow twigs, and the pastry which you eat is made of paste, which your mother rolled out on a wooden board with a wooden rolling-pin.

As you come out from school you get a lift in a farm-cart, that too is made of wood, and so is the wheelbarrow you use, when you get home, for wheeling manure into the garden. You put your school things away in the old oak-chest in the corner, and when you go to bed after supper, you look up at the old beams across the ceiling and fall asleep dreaming of wood everywhere.

You could add many more things that I have forgotten; and even now we have not reckoned up the gums, the turpentine, the oils, the tannin, and the many sweet scents which we get from trees. Nor have we spoken of boats, and railway carriages, nor of the beautiful wood-carvings in our churches and other public buildings. Surely the world would get on very badly without trees!

Name any things made of wood besides those given in the lesson.

CHAPTER II

HOW A TREE STARTS

WE saw in Book III. that some plants live much longer than others. Some live for one year only, make their seeds and die. These we call *annuals*. Others live two years. They grow their roots and leaves one year, and flower and make their seeds the next year. These we call *biennials*, because *bi* means two. Others live for many years, and are called *perennials*. Trees are perennials, for they live for very many years. There are some oak trees more than a thousand years old.

Yet all these old trees began their lives as little seedlings, like the bean you grew on the top of the earth in the flower-pot. How, then, have they managed to live so long? We shall learn this best by looking at a young seedling.

If you poke about in a wood, you will easily find some small plant, either of oak, or beech, or hazel, which has grown up from a nut, or an acorn trodden into the ground. I am going to take an oak tree, because I have one close to my door and can give you a picture of it. If you get an acorn and stick it in the neck of a bottle, the same way up as it sits in its cup, and keep the bottle full of water, you can grow a small oak for yourself, and see if yours is like mine.

First the acorn puts out some roots downwards. Then the husk splits, and you can see the two thick seed-leaves open, with the growing tip between them. This tip now grows steadily upwards and soon puts forth leaves. There may be one, or even two, one above the other, on the sides of the stem. But there will certainly be two or three close together at the top of the little tree by the time autumn comes. At the foot of each leaf, nestling up to the stem, will be a little bud, and at the end of the stem will be a stout bud, bigger than all the rest.

The difference between the oak-plant and the bean which we grew in Book III. is that the stem is woody. If you get another oak-plant of the same age from the wood, and cut off its head this is what you will see (Fig. 1, p. 7). In the middle there is a round white patch, *p.* This is the *pith*, or soft part, which you scoop out of the branch of

YOUNG OAK PLANT
1. Growth of 1st Year
2. Growth of 2nd Year
3. Growth of 3rd Year
r. Ring left by scales of buds

HOW A TREE STARTS

an elder-tree when you make a popgun. Next comes a ring of soft whitish *wood, w.* Outside this again is the *bark, b.*

Now you know that water, with earthy matter in it, has to rise up from the roots and go to the leaves, to be made into food. It travels up through this ring of living wood, and when it comes back it makes new wood and new bark just where the wood and the bark meet. You know how easy it is to peel the bark off wood. That is because the tender new part is between them, and gives way easily.

But as soon as autumn comes, the roots leave off taking in water; and the crude *sap*, as it is called, does not rise up any more. The stalks of the leaves dry up where they join the stem, and they fall off. The tree rests for the winter.

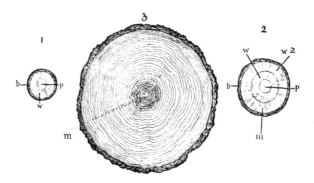

OAK STEMS CUT ACROSS
1. Twig of 1st year   2. Twig of 2nd year
3. Trunk of an old Oak with rings of growth
p. pith   *w.* wood   *b.* bark
w2. Wood of the 2nd year   *m.* Medullary or Pith ray

Now watch your little plant next spring. You will see the big bud at the tip, and often two other buds close to it, begin to grow into branches and have leaves of their own. But in a very young tree the smaller ones usually die away and the trunk grows straight up. However, you can always tell where the new growth began in the spring, because there is a ring (r, p. 6) left by the scales of the buds. The wood of the new piece will be just like the wood of the lower piece was last year. But that lower piece will be growing some fresh wood and getting bigger (Fig. 2, p. 7). The sap will go up and down as before, and a new ring of wood ($w\,2$) will form *outside* the old wood, and a very thin new ring of bark *inside* the old bark. So at the end of the second year, while the new piece will have only one ring of wood, the old piece below the scales will have two rings *(w and $w\,2$)*, with a mark between the rings, showing where the tree rested in the winter.

All this is rather difficult to see in such small trees, and you must look at the diagrams. But if you go into the wood when they are cutting down timber, you will see the rings much more distinctly in the older trees, and you will like to look at the trunks, and try to make out how old the trees are. You cannot be quite sure that you count all the years, because as the new wood grows, the old is squeezed together, and makes a very hard wood, called "heart-wood," in the middle of the trunk. But you can be sure that the tree is not

HOW A TREE STARTS

younger, and most likely much older, than the rings you can count.

Now to come back to our question, how trees live to be so old. Year after year they make a new ring of wood, narrower and narrower as they grow older. Through the younger rings the crude sap goes up to the leaves, and the food-sap comes down to feed the parts of the tree. Buds are formed every spring on the stems at the foot of each leaf, and these buds are like new plants. They start with fresh strength, making new food for the tree, which carries them up on its trunk and branches into the light and air.

The heart-wood of the tree is really dead, and sometimes decays away while the outer part of the tree is still flourishing. But many of the rings of wood far inside the trunk still want food, and if you look at a felled tree you can see how they get it. Besides the rings, you will see some lines *(m)*, like the spokes of a wheel, starting from the centre of the trunk and spreading out to the bark. These lines are made of pith, like that we saw in the middle of the young seedling oak. Until they are squeezed away the sap passes along them all through the tree.

There are some trees, such as the palms, which you see in hot-houses, which do not grow in rings. But these are not English, and do not concern us here.

Get several pieces of tree-branches and try to see the bark, the inner bark, the rings of wood and the heart-wood—Lilac,

TREES AND SHRUBS

Lime, and Elder show the parts well. Oak and Pine show heartwood best.

CHAPTER III

HOW A TREE GROWS—
THE HORSE-CHESTNUT

When a young tree has made plenty of wood and branches, it begins to use some of its buds for making flowers. These buds grow in the same places as leaf-buds. In some trees they grow where the leaf joins the stem. In others they grow at the tips of the twigs. They are generally rounder and less pointed than the leaf-buds.

The flowers of the oak are very small, so you had better look out for a horse-chestnut tree and gather a bough for this lesson. You will find buds on a horse-chestnut tree almost any time in the year, except when it is in full leaf, and then they will be very small.

The best time to look is just at the end of the winter, when the tree is bare. First notice the smaller buds, which grow two and two opposite each other along the twig. You will see below each bud a scar marking the place on which the leaf grew last year. This scar is shaped like a horseshoe, and has several black spots on it arranged like the nails. These spots show where the bundles of tubes were, which carried the sap into the leaf.

Now pick one of the buds to pieces. They are small, and you will not find it very easy, but you can take off the brown sticky scales, and you will find inside, first some soft gummy down, and then the young green leaves, tightly folded together, with a green growing tip between them.

So if you had left that bud, and it could get food enough, it would have grown into a small branch in the spring, with leaves on it. But it is very seldom that *all* the buds on a branch grow. The stronger ones take the food, and the weaker ones either die or wait till next year.

Now look at the buds on the tips of the branches. They are very much larger than those growing on the sides, and you can examine them easily. When you have taken away from twelve to seventeen sticky scales, you will come to the same kind of soft white gummy down which you found in the leaf-buds, making a warm bed for the tender growing parts inside.

But this bud is not all leaves like the smaller one. It has four small bright green leaves, and wrapped up inside them is a tiny spike covered with little knobs (F).

You cannot examine the flowers on this spike without a microscope. But if you wait and watch till

HOW A TREE GROWS — THE HORSE CHESTNUT

May, you will see others like it gradually opening out into a lovely branch of flowers, and I think you will like them all the better for knowing how the tree prepared them last autumn, when it was covered with leaves, and wrapped them up warm all the winter in sticky buds.

And while you are waiting for the flowers, look at the tree itself. The trunk is smooth and round. The branches begin to grow out of it about ten feet from the ground. They grow two and two opposite to each other like the leaves, except where a bud has failed. The lower branches, which of course are the oldest, stretch out farthest, so that the tree rounds off very gracefully up to the top.

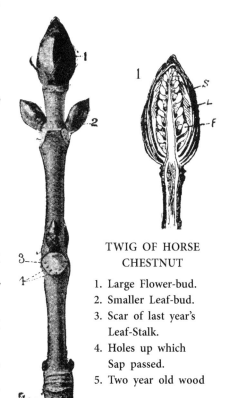

TWIG OF HORSE CHESTNUT
1. Large Flower-bud.
2. Smaller Leaf-bud.
3. Scar of last year's Leaf-Stalk.
4. Holes up which Sap passed.
5. Two year old wood

FLOWER-BUD
S. Covering Scales
L. Folded Leaves
F. Flowers not yet opened

Then, as April comes, the brown scales fall from the leaf-buds, and the tree is covered with bright green downy leaves. They are each cut into seven leaflets, which hang down from the tip of the leaf-stalk like a half-opened umbrella. Little by little, as they grow stronger, they rise up into a broad leaf with seven fingers. It is while they are doing this that the flower-buds throw off their scales, the four green leaves open out, and the flower spike begins to hang out its snow-white flowers, streaked with pink and yellow (opposite).

The flowers nearest to the branch open first and grow strong. They are perfect flowers, with five green sepals and five beautiful crimped petals, and have both stamens and seed-box inside. These will form the chestnuts which ripen in the autumn. The flowers nearer to the tip of the spike have only stamens inside the petals. They wither away as soon as they have shed their pollen-dust.

If you can get an old flower spike when the flowers are withered, and cut the seed-box of a flower across, you will see that it has three divisions with two little seeds in each. But when you pick up the prickly fruit in the autumn, though it burst into three parts, there are generally only two horse-chestnuts inside, with another very tiny one. The two big seeds have starved out the other four little ones and grown big and strong. If the chestnuts are brown and shiny, they are ripe, and will grow if you sow them.

Though the horse-chestnut is very beautiful in the summer, its leaves turn yellow very early and fall in

HORSE-CHESTNUT FLOWER AND FRUIT

TREES AND SHRUBS

August, and then you can see the buds already formed for next year. All boys know that horse-chestnuts are bitter and not good eating. The sweet chestnuts, which we roast, come from quite a different tree, and are not seeds, but fruits.

Bring a branch of horse-chestnut and examine the buds. Find a flower spike in May; look at the ovary in June, and the fruit in September.

CHAPTER IV

TREES WITH CATKIN FLOWERS

THE horse-chestnut is the only big English tree which has large flower-spikes. There are many pretty flowering shrubs in the hedge, such as the Blackthorn, the May, and the Guelder rose. But all the big trees have tiny flowers. As some of these trees flower before they open their leaves, you can see their blossoms. So we will look at a few.

If you live where there are many bees, and where there are any trees of the common Sallow Willow growing in the hedges, or the woods, go out some sunny day in March, and lie down under one of the trees and listen.

Before long you will bear a buzzing, which will go on as long as the sun is bright. For the bees have wakened from their long winter sleep, and want honey and pollen to make bee-bread. There are very few flowers open in March and, as the sweet smell of honey comes from the blossoms of the willow, the bees are quick to find them out.

Perhaps you will ask me how you are to know

a Sallow Willow. You know it quite well, though you may not know the name. It is a big shrubby tree, with a purple-brown stem, which grows in the hedges and woods, and from which people cut branches before Palm Sunday, and call them palms.

All up the twigs you will see in March and April round soft bodies about as big as thimbles growing now on one side now on the other. It is into these that the bees are poking their heads. You remember the catkins which we saw on the nut-trees in Book I. These soft bodies clinging close to the willow stems are also catkins. In willows they stand up, instead of hanging down as they do on the nut-trees, and on the sallow willow they hug the stem.

But now I want you to look a little further. The tree under which you sit may have broad yellow catkins (2, opposite), and if you gather a branch and look closely at it, you will see the yellow anthers standing out all round the catkin. Children call these "golden palms." But you may find, not so very far away, another of the same kind of tree, on which the catkins are soft and grey (1, opposite). They are much longer and narrower than the golden catkins. Children call them "silver pussy-palms."

Gather a branch from each of these trees and take them to school. When you pick them to pieces, you will find that each catkin is made up of a number of tiny flowers. In the golden catkins each flower is

SALLOW WILLOW

TREES AND SHRUBS

only a little scaly leaf *(L, 2)* with two stamens growing on it. No! I forgot. There is something else, for at the bottom of each scaly leaf is a small cup *(H)*, holding a drop of honey. So you see there are plenty of drops of honey in a catkin.

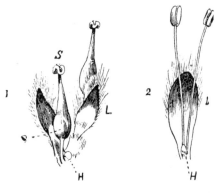

FLOWERS OF THE SALLOW WILLOW
1. Flower with Ovary
2. Flower with Stamens
L. Leaf-scale   H. Honey-cup
O. Ovary   S. Stigma

Then if you pick the silver-pussy-palm to pieces, you will find the same honey cup *(H)* at the bottom of the scale, but instead of stamens, there is a little seed-box or ovary *(O)* shaped like a bottle, with a crumpled stigma *(S)*.

Now you see the use of the honey. As the dust-bags and the seed-boxes are on different trees, the flowers have to tempt the bees to carry the pollen. It is wise to plant willows near where bees are kept, for they get plenty of honey from them in the spring. The Osier willow, which grows in the marshes, and is used for making baskets, is in bloom at the same time as the sallow. But the common English willow which grows into a large tree, and the Crack willow whose branches break off so easily when you bend them, bloom later, when their narrow pointed leaves are out. They all bloom early,

TREES WITH CATKIN FLOWERS

however, and when the tiny seeds covered with down are blown out of the catkins many a little bird uses them to line its nest.

Another tree, which blooms before its leaves come, is the English poplar, which grows by the streams, or in the woods. Poplars have their two kinds of flowers on different trees, like the willows. But they have no honey, and no bees come near them. I think that if you have any poplars in your woods and watch them, you will guess how they manage. For when the wild March winds are blowing, the long hanging catkins swing to and fro, and the dry pollen-dust is blown through the air from tree to tree.

I wonder if you know which tree I mean by the English poplar? Not those tall stiff trees which point straight up to the sky. Those come from Italy and are called Lombardy poplars. The English poplars are graceful trees with very broad leaves hanging on long stalks. The white poplar has soft white hairs under its leaves, and the leaves of the aspen or trembling poplar are silky underneath. The leaves turn on their long stalks when the wind blows and look very pretty as they show their white sides.

One other tree you must look for, which has its stamens in long loose catkins and its ovary in a little bud with scales round it. This is our friend the oak after it has grown into a large tree. The oak flowers in the spring, just as the leaves are coming out. You will easily

TREES AND SHRUBS

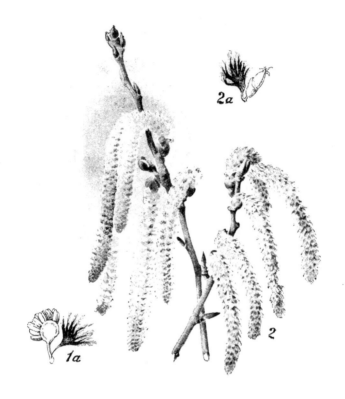

TWIGS OF ENGLISH POPLAR

1. Catkins with Anther Flowers   1a. One Flower enlarged
2. Catkins with ovary-bearing Flowers   2a. One Flower enlarged

see the catkins waving in the wind, but the flowers which will grow into acorns are very small and grow singly, or in pairs, between the leaf-stalk and the stem. Each one has a number of small scales round it, which by-and-by will harden into the cup of the acorn.

TREES WITH CATKIN FLOWERS

But the oak is such an important tree that we must talk of it in a separate lesson.

Bring willow branches in March with stamen-catkins, and others with seed-forming catkins. Look for the honey cup. Bring leaves and flowers of the English poplar.

CHAPTER V

THE BRITISH OAK

I wonder if you have any woods near you with oak trees growing close together, or mixed with beech and ash trees. This is the way they are grown, when they are to be cut into long planks, or poles, and most likely there will be some wood, where you can stop and look at them on your way home from school.

They will have straight, smooth trunks; some twenty, some thirty, some perhaps fifty feet high, before the branches spread out above. Yet you know that your seedling oak has buds, first on one side, then on the other, all up the stem. How is it that these buds have not grown into branches?

The reason is that in a thick wood, where the trees crowd each other, every tree wants to raise its head up to the light. So in the spring when the leaves and buds open out at the top of the little tree, and the crude sap rises up to them from the roots, the tree wants so much to use for growing up higher that only a small quantity goes down again to make new wood. So the buds lower down do not get enough food to grow,

THE BRITISH OAK

and they either die or become dormant. That is, they remain waiting for another opportunity, which often never comes. For this reason oaks in a wood grow taller and taller with only a crown of branches and leaves near the top.

But if you can find an old oak out in the open field, or at the edge of the wood, where it has plenty of room, you will see that it has grown differently. The trunk is much larger, and the branches grow out lower down. In many big oaks a man can reach the lower boughs as he stands under it. The branches are very heavy and stretch out widely all round, so that an old oak tree covers a great deal of space in open ground. If the trunk were not very strong it could not bear the weight of such huge branches. But it is very broad at the bottom and then curves in and rises like a stout pillar till it becomes broad again where the branches divide away from it.

When Smeaton, the great engineer, built the Eddystone lighthouse, he shaped it like the trunk of an oak, and the lighthouse stood firm against wind and waves for more than a hundred years.

The oak has a very thick strong root from which long ropy roots run out all round the tree. I will tell you a way by which you may know how far the roots of a tree spread underground. Look at the branches and see how far they stretch out from the trunk, for the roots will reach just as far underground as the branches do above ground.

The reason of this is very interesting. You will remember that the tips of the roots are the mouths of a plant. They drink in the water. Now when it rains, the raindrops trickle from leaf to leaf till they come to the tips of the branches, and then they drip down and sink into the ground. The roots would get very little rain-water if they stopped under the tree where you and I stand to keep out of the rain. But as the tree grows, the roots find their way farther and farther out, till they reach the place where the drip will be.

You will find it useful to know this in gardening and farming, for tree roots are often very troublesome.

When you have looked at the rugged bark of the old oak, which is so useful for tanning leather, look up at the branches. They twist and turn in all directions, and there is a very thick joint wherever a new branch starts.

You can see the reason of this, if you look at your young tree (p. 6), or at a twig of the old tree. There is not one bud at the tip of the twigs as there was in the horse-chestnut, but two, three, or sometimes more. All these buds crowd each other, and the middle one generally dies. The others go off different ways, and so make what carpenters call "knee-joints." These were used for shipbuilding in olden days, because they are very strong. But now that ships are made of iron, knee-timber is not so much wanted, and straight planks and poles are more valuable. So it is best now to plant oaks in woods, where their stems grow straight and smooth.

Oak timber has always been valuable. The beams of Westminster Hall, which was built about nine hundred years ago, are made of Durmast Oak, and are still as good as ever. Many country cottages have old chests and carved chairs in them quite as old as this. The heartwood of the oak is very firm and strong, and this is why the old song says

CATKINS OF THE OAK

> "Hearts of Oak are our ships,
> Hearts of Oak are our Men."

You can see the trunk and branches of the oak best, in winter. Then when April is nearly over, a pretty crimson colour comes on all the buds, the leaves open out, and the loose catkins hang down between them, while the tiny acorn flowers nestle between the leaf-stalk and the stem.

When the leaves are fully out, and the acorns are beginning to form, try if you can find the two kinds of English oak. Their leaves are much the same shape,

OAK BRANCHES WITH ACORNS

1. Common Oak with stalked Acorns
2. Durmast Oak with Acorns close to the Branch

THE BRITISH OAK

long and cut into deep divisions. But the leaves of the Common Oak (1, opposite) have very short leaf-stalks, they almost touch the stem, while the acorns stand on long stalks. In the other tree called the Durmast Oak the leaves usually have longer stalks, and the acorns have none.

The evergreen oak, which is often grown in gardens, was brought from Italy. Its leaves are something like the leaves of the holly, so it is called the holm oak or holly oak.

Get a branch of oak and notice the crowded buds. Get a log of oak and notice the dark heartwood and the rings round it. Also the rugged bark. Try to find the two kinds of English oak. Notice the scales grown together in the acorn cup.

CHAPTER VI

GUESTS OF THE OAK

THE oak feeds more creatures than any other English tree. Not only do the pigs, the hedgehogs, the squirrels, and the field-mice feed on the acorns, but more than fifty kinds of insects get their food from some part of the tree.

Many of these are too small for you to find, but you will enjoy looking out for others. If you examine an oak-tree in May, you will most likely find some of its leaves rolled up, either from the tip towards the stalk, or from side to side. Undo this roll and you will find a caterpillar inside, or perhaps a chrysalis. There are two kinds of caterpillars which roll up oak leaves. One, which is called simply the Oak-moth caterpillar, is large. It rolls up the leaf rather untidily, and spins a cocoon round itself inside, in the shape of a little boat. The moth when it comes out has bright green wings with two white bands on them.

The other caterpillar, which you are almost sure to find, does its work more tidily. It makes a very neat roll, and fastens it together with fine threads. Then it feeds on the inner rolls till it goes to sleep, and turns into a moth. If you shake an oak-tree in June numbers of these little moths will often fly out. They are called the Green Oak-moth, though their hind wings are brown. They are much smaller than the oak-moth, whose caterpillar spins the boat cocoon.

Another insect which you may find, is the grub of the great Stag Beetle. For this you will have to cut into the trunks of old trees, where the big grub hollows out a bed for itself under the bark. It stays there and feeds on the wood of the tree for three or four years, till it turns into the beetle. You remember that the woodpecker taps with his beak as he climbs the trees. It is grubs like these that he is trying to find.

OAK LEAVES ROLLED UP WITH CHRYSALIS INSIDE

But the most curious homes on an oak-tree are the galls made by mother insects, which lay their eggs on some part of the tree. Every country child knows the red-brown rosy-cheeked oak-apple, which grows on the tips of the oak-twigs, and which many people mistake for fruit. Boys used to stick these in their hats on the twenty-ninth of May, because Charles the Second, who hid from his enemies in an oak-tree, came back to his throne on that day.

Instead of sticking it into your caps, cut the oak-apple across with a sharp knife. You will find that it is soft and spongy, and is divided into a number of small cells. In each of these cells there will be either a grub, or a cocoon, or a perfect fly ready to come out. Or perhaps the home may be empty, all the inmates having flown away.

OAK-APPLE. INSECT CELLS SEEN IN THE APPLE CUT OPEN

Let us see how this oak-apple came to be there. Early in the spring a small wasp-fly, called a Cynips, settled on the twig, and pierced the bark with a sharp-pointed tube. She carries this tube coiled up at the end of her body, till she wants to use it. Then she darts it out into the twig and squeezes some juice into the hole, together with several eggs.

GUESTS OF THE OAK

In a very short time a swelling rises up, and the spongy oak-apple grows round the eggs, each one being in a cell by itself. So when the grubs are hatched they find plenty of soft food to eat, till they spin their cocoons.

OAK GALLS
1. Artichoke Galls   2. Oak-spangles
3. Currant galls   4. Hard brown Oak-gall

Another of these flies lays its eggs on the loose catkins. You may easily find them hanging like little brown currants on the stalk (3, p. 33), after the flowers have withered. For though the stalk falls off as a rule, yet when these galls are on it, it remains hanging till the fly comes out.

These "currant galls" have each one grub in them, and so too have the galls which you will find under the leaves. There are at least two kinds of leaf-galls. One is bright red, and is called a "cherry gall." The other is very small, pink, hairy, and flat. There are a great many of these under each leaf, and they are called "oak-spangles" (2, p. 33). The grub remains in these galls after the leaves have fallen, so you will be able to find them.

The next gall (1, p. 33) I am sure you will think is a bud. It is called the "artichoke gall," and really begins in the oak-bud, in which the fly lays her eggs early in the spring. Then instead of growing into a twig with green leaves, the bud covers itself with scales, and a number of grubs are hatched inside.

Last of all there are the big brown galls, specially called "oak-galls" (4, p. 33). They grow half-way down the twigs, and remain hanging on the tree all the winter, after the flies have flown out. This gall was first seen in England about sixty years ago, in 1840. It has spread very fast, and is hurtful to the trees, for it sucks out a great deal of sap. It is very like the galls which we get

1. BEECH TREE 2. MAST, OR BEECH NUT
3. SWEET CHESTNUT 4. NUTS IN THE HUSK

from Asia, in order to use the acid in them for making ink.

Many other trees have galls on them besides the oak, and I advise you when you find a curious lump or a strange-shaped bud, unlike anything you expect to find on a tree, to cut it open and see if there is a grub inside.

Find as many different kinds of oak-gall as you can. Find the leaf-rolling caterpillars, and try to find the grub of the stag-beetle.

CHAPTER VII

THE BEECH AND THE SWEET CHESTNUT

As you go through the woods in spring, you should watch the trees when they break out into leaf. One of the prettiest is the Beech Tree (1, plate, p. 35), You may know it in the middle of winter by its olive-grey bark, its tall, smooth trunk with a broad crown of branches on the top, and its brown sharp-pointed buds which grow one after the other, now on one side, now on the other of the stem. How different they are from the thick buds of the horse-chestnut, and yet they keep the little leaves inside quite as safe and warm.

Pick one of them to pieces in the early spring, just before they burst open (*see* p. 38). You will find, first, a number of shiny brown scales folded tight one over the other. Then inside these, some transparent scales as soft as silk, wrapping round the delicate tiny leaves which are folded up like a fan, and have a fringe of silvery hairs on them. Lastly, in the middle, the tender growing tip lies safely hidden.

A few days later these bright green leaves will

open, and the scales hang loosely below them, while the silken fringe now shows as hairs under the leaves. Each leaf is oval and notched at the edge, and the twigs on which they grow droop at first, and then slowly raise themselves. By the time the leaves are full grown the brown clusters of flowers are hanging among them.

Those with the stamens in them are soft and silky, and hang on long, thin stalks; but those with the seed-boxes, stand up on short stalks near the end of the twigs. There are two or three of them on each stalk, with their sticky horns standing up, and a number of prickly scales round them.

BEECH BUDS IN WINTER
The top Bud is stripped of its Brown Scales.

These scales are like those we saw round the acorn. They grow into a hard husk covered with prickles, and by-and-by quite shut in the two or three little nuts. But when autumn comes, the "beech-mast" (2, p. 35), as it is called, falls down, the husk bursts open into four pieces, and then you see inside the three-cornered nuts with the withered horns still on the top.

THE BEECH AND THE SWEET CHESTNUT

Now, why do you think these scales grow into such a hard husk and shut in the fruit, and why do they burst in the autumn? Because the squirrels and field-mice feed chiefly on beech-nuts, and if there were no husk to protect the nuts while they are green, they would be eaten before they were ripe. But now the husk falls and bursts, just when they are ready to grow. The tree can spare a good many to be eaten, if the squirrels and other animals tread a few into the ground or bury them so that they grow. Beech trees spring up so well from seed that there is no need to plant them. But if you want to keep a beech wood healthy and cut it down for timber you must take care of it. The trees live for more than two hundred years, though they are ready to be cut down when they are about ninety years old.

Good foresters cut down one block at a time, so that there is always some part of the wood getting ready for timber. In the part they are going to cut, they first clear away the other kinds of trees and the young stunted beeches, so as to let in the light and air.

Then they wait for a year or two, till there comes a season when the beech-mast is good, and the seeds are strong and will grow well. This happens generally about every three or four years. Then they begin to thin out the trees for timber, and so to leave room for young seedlings to grow up and begin a new crop.

After this they go on cutting down some every year, and clear that piece of the wood in about ten years or more. By that time the new beech-trees have a good crown of branches and leaves on the top and go on and grow, while the forester begins to cut down another part of the wood.

If the beech-tree is pretty in spring, it is still more lovely in the autumn, when its leaves turn a bright red, and by-and-by fall and make a lovely carpet of leaves in the wood. The young beech-trees keep their dead leaves on all through the winter, and so do beech-hedges, which are kept cut and not allowed to grow into trees.

There is another tree you know well, which shuts up its fruit in a husk made of prickly scales. This is the sweet or Spanish chestnut (3, p. 35), which the Romans brought to our country, and which now grows in the woods, or is often planted in the avenues leading to big houses. It opens its leaves later than the beech, and does not bloom till July. Still by October the nuts are ripe, and the husks burst open on the ground. And when you pick up the nuts to take them home to roast, you may notice the dry remains of the flower making a kind of bristling fringe on their points (4, p. 35). Quite late in the autumn the chestnut is a lovely tree. Its long narrow leaves, cut in sharp points at the edge turn a beautiful golden brown and hang on a long time.

Many beams of old houses are made of chestnut, and the trunks of the young trees are made into hop-poles. Beech-wood is used very largely for making chairs.

THE BEECH AND THE SWEET CHESTNUT

The Birch and the Alder are both trees with catkins and hard-shelled fruits like the beech and the oak. They flower in the early spring before the leaves are fully out. The alder grows near streams or on wet ground. The birch you will find in the woods, and know it by its slender, graceful trunk, marked with brown, yellow and silvery streaks, its purple-brown twigs, and its dark green leaves—these smell very strong after rain, because the resin oozes from them. Some diseased birches have large tufts of twigs growing on the upper branches, looking like crows' nests.

Bring, in spring, a beech branch with its buds. Bring, in autumn, beech-nuts and chestnuts in their husks. Compare a chestnut, which is a fruit, with a horse chestnut, which is a seed. Find Birch and Alder fruits.

CHAPTER VIII

TREES WHICH BEAR CONES

Pines, firs, and larches grow in almost all parts of England. They are very interesting and useful trees. They all form their seeds in woody cones, and their leaves are very narrow or needle-shaped, quite unlike the leaves of most other trees.

A large part of the timber we use comes from pines and firs, grown in Norway and other countries. It is called pine-wood and deal. No doubt you have noticed the small round pieces called "knots" in deal, and have poked them out, leaving a hole. These are places where branches grew and broke off, and then the trunk closed round them; they are common in deal and pinewood. The sap in these trees is very resinous and they are tapped for turpentine. If you walk in a pine wood, or crush the leaves of a pine or fir, you will notice the strong scent of this resinous juice.

Every country child has picked up fir cones, and you may easily find three different kinds, those belonging to the Scotch pine, the Spruce fir, and the Larch. Of these three, only the Scotch pine is a native

TREES WHICH BEAR CONES

of Great Britain, the other two have been brought from abroad.

There were once dense forests of Scotch pine in England, but these have been cut down long ago, and the pine woods we have now, have grown up from the seeds of trees brought from the great forests in Scotland, Norway, and France. It is a tall tree with spreading branches and a trunk covered with a red or brown scaly bark. Perhaps you know it as Scotch fir, for people confuse these two names, and call the same tree "pine" or "fir," though you may know the difference if you look at the cones.

The dark-green leaves of the Scotch pine are very narrow, and about two inches long (*see* p. 44). They grow *two together* in a sheath of brown scales. Its cones have no stalks, and they bulge out at the bottom, and taper away to a blunt point at the upper end. They are made of a number of thick woody scales which look as if they were folded back at the top, making a solid thick knob with a brown scaly spot where the tip ends (*see* p. 44). These scales fit over each other so tightly that, before the cone is ripe, not even a drop of rain can get in, and they take two or three years to ripen. Sometimes they hang all the time on the tree. Sometimes they fall off earlier. As they ripen, the woody scales bend outwards and you can see two thin, transparent scales inside each, which look like the wings of a fly. They stand upright against the woody scale.

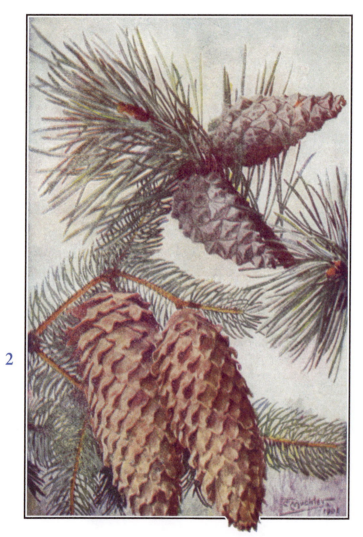

1. SCOTCH PINE AND CONES   2. SPRUCE FIR AND CONES

TREES WHICH BEAR CONES

Slip a knife carefully down under these, right to the bottom and pull them out. You will find a seed at the end of each, if you have not broken the tender translucent membrane.

For these are winged seeds, which have no seed-box over them, but grow naked inside the woody scale. After a time they fall out and are blown away by the wind. If you get a cone that is too old they will be gone.

All trees with cones have these winged seeds, and the cones of true pines are very much alike. You will easily know the Cluster pine, which has been brought from France and is found in many English woods among the Scotch pines. Its large cones grow in clusters round the branches, four or sometimes eight, together. They are larger and browner than the cones of the Scotch pine and they often remain a great many years on the tree.

The Spruce *fir* (2, opposite) is very different from the Scotch *pine*. Its spreading branches grow nearly down to the ground, and its needle-shaped leaves, which are barely an inch long grow *singly* on the stem. Its cones are long and narrow and the scales are not so thick as in pines. But the chief difference is that the *tips are not bent back* into knobs, they are pointed and bend in a little, and by this you may know fir-cones from pine-cones.

The firs have two seeds inside each scale like the

pine, but these ripen in one year. The spruce fir came from Norway, and now grows all over England.

The Larch, which came from Switzerland, and the Cedar, which came from Lebanon in Palestine, both grow their seeds in cones, but they are rather different from the pines and firs. Their needle-leaves are very thin and grow in *tufts* eighteen or twenty together in the same sheath of scales. The cones of the cedar stand upright and are shaped like an egg, but the tree does not often bear cones in England.

LARCH TWIG BEARING CONES

Larch cones are quite small, not more than an inch in length; they grow along the twigs in a row. The woody scales do not fit very tightly together.

I think you can find the cones of all these trees except the cedar. Of course you must look for fir and larch cones in the autumn, because they ripen each year, but pine-cones are on the trees all the year round. If you look at any of these trees in the spring and early summer, you will see their stamen-catkins hanging

TREES WHICH BEAR CONES

from the branches, and the yellow pollen blowing about in clouds so as to fall on the young cones.

Pines, firs, and cedars are evergreen trees. Their leaves remain on the tree three years or more; and as the branches are not of the same age, the leaves fall off in different years, so that the trees are always green. But the larch sheds its leaves every year, and you may easily know it, in the autumn by its bare drooping boughs covered with small brown cones.

Pines and firs will flourish in very poor soil and their seeds grow up easily. If you are near a pine wood, or a wood of mixed trees with pines or firs in it, try and find a seedling tree. It is curious to look at, for it shoots up with a long, thin stalk, and carries up the seed-coat with it. When this coat falls off, you see five or six long seed-leaves underneath, and in the middle of them a bud with the real pine or fir leaves.

TWIGS OF YEW
1. With Flowers in spring
2. With red Cup and Seed in Autumn

TREES AND SHRUBS

There is another tree which you know well, which has needle-shaped leaves. They grow all round the stem, two together in each sheath, but they are flattened down on two sides of the stem like the featherlets of a feather. This is the Yew tree (*see* p. 47), which you find so often in church-yards. It does not bear cones. Its naked seeds sit each one in a red juicy cup. The stamen-catkins are not on the same tree as the red cups, but if you search well you will find them on another yew tree.

Bring in a bunch of the Scotch pine and the Spruce fir. Compare the cones of the two trees. Try to find a branch of Cedar, a branch of the Larch with cones, a seedling pine or fir, a branch of Yew with stamen flowers in March, and another with the red cup and naked seed in the autumn.

CHAPTER IX

HEDGEROW SHRUBS AND TREES

THERE is no country in the world where the hedgerows are so beautiful as in England. Whether we look at the neatly trimmed hedges round our gardens, or the roughly-trimmed fences between the fields, they each have their beauty. Perhaps the most delightful of all, to look at, are the hedges which are not cut more than once in six years. But these are not good for the fields.

Let us look first at the garden hedges. Have you ever thought that these are all made of young trees, clipped so that they remain only branches and leaves, and do not grow tall trunks? A box hedge is made of box trees closely cut. The holly hedge, whose prickly leaves are so useful in preventing the cattle from breaking through, would grow into tall trees if left alone. I know a garden in Devonshire where there are holly trees thirty feet high, growing here and there in a holly hedge.

The hawthorn fence is the same as the May-tree which grows on the lawn. The beech hedge is made of beech trees, kept well clipped, and the dead leaves hang on it in winter, as they do on young beeches. The yew hedge is the same as the big yew tree in the churchyard, and it is well to be careful how you plant it anywhere near cattle and horses, for in a hard winter they sometimes eat the poisonous leaves and die.

But each of these hedges is made of only one kind of tree. They are not nearly so interesting as the mixed hedges which grow between the fields. There we find blackberries and nuts and all sorts of curious fruits and flowers.

Do you know the Blackthorn bush, whose small white flowers grow on its black stem, almost before winter is over and while it has no leaves? If you do, I expect you know that you will find purple sloes on it in the autumn, under its small dark-green leaves, and you can gather the fruit to make sloe syrup or sloe wine. The blackthorn is not a good hedge plant, for its roots wander far out into the field, and it often grows into a tree and so leaves a gap in the fence.

The Hawthorn or May is much better, for it grows into a thick quickset hedge, if it is properly cut, and the cattle do not break through it, because of its thorns. But you cannot use the fruit of the hawthorn, you must leave the haws for the birds.

Then, in the hedge, or the wood, you will most likely find the Crab-apple tree, with its spreading branches, often covered with thorns. It has oval leaves with sharp points, which are downy underneath when they are young. Its rosy pink-and-white blossoms come out in May, and in the autumn you will find the red crab-apple in their place. This fruit is sour and bitter.

1. BIRD CHERRY   2. GUELDER ROSE

Another hedgerow tree is the Wild Cherry, whose fruit feeds the birds in the summer, and helps to keep them away from the corn. It is a bushy shrub with a red bark and blue-green egg-shaped leaves, very much notched round the edge. Its flowers grow on short stalks four or five from one point like our garden cherries, and the fruit, when it is ripe, is a bright red. If you live in Wales, or the middle or north of England, you may find

(BELOW) ROWAN TREE   (ABOVE) SPINDLE TREE

another tree called the Bird-cherry (1, p. 51), whose flowers grow along a thin stalk, and its fruit is black. But be sure you find the right one with long, drooping flower clusters, for many people call the wild dwarf cherry by this name.

The blackthorn, hawthorn, crab-apple, and cherry all belong to the rose family, which, you remember, has so many fruit-bearing plants in it. So does the pretty Rowan tree (plate, opposite), often called the Mountain Ash, because its leaves are cut into leaflets very like those of the ash-tree. You will find the small white flowers of the Rowan tree (l, opposite) open in May. But you will like it best in autumn when the clusters of beautiful red berries are ripe. Perhaps you have one over your gate, for they were often planted there when people believed in witches, as they were supposed to keep them away.

I must find room to tell you of two more hedgerow shrubs. One is the Guelder Rose (2, p. 51), which has dark-green leaves cut into three or five points with a jagged edge. These leaves turn a lovely red in the autumn. Its white flowers grow in a flat cluster. The outer ones are large and have neither stamens nor seed-box in them. Their use is to attract the bees and flies, which come to the smaller flowers in the middle to fetch honey. These middle flowers are perfect and so the insects help them to form seed. The guelder rose has beautiful coral-red berries in the autumn.

TREES AND SHRUBS

The other bush, which grows about five feet high in the hedge, is called the Spindle tree (2, p. 52), because its wood is used for making spindles and skewers. It has a smooth, grey stem and narrow, green leaves, which are very poisonous. You will scarcely notice its small green-white flowers in May. But in the autumn it has a lovely and curious fruit. Four red seed-boxes grow together in a clump on a short stalk. They look very quaint, and if you open them you will find that the seed inside is covered with a bright orange-coloured membrane.

Find the flowers and fruit of the blackthorn, may, apple and wild cherry, rowan tree, guelder rose, and spindle tree.

CHAPTER X

GARDEN SHRUBS IN BLOOM

THERE is not room to grow large trees in a cottage garden, but many flowering shrubs can be planted in corners, and some of them are very lovely. The first to bloom in the year is the Japan pear, *Pyrus japonica (see* p. 59). It grows on many cottage walls, and makes them bright when the trees are bare of leaves. Its deep-red buds are showing even in January, and by the end of February the wall is covered with them. They are like pear blossoms in shape, and grow in little bunches close against the stem. If you have not got one you will easily find a sucker, growing out from some neighbour's plant, and it is not difficult to rear. In the autumn you will see its hard, green fruit.

Soon after the Japan pear is in full bloom the *Ribes*, or "flowering currant," will be showing its red tassels in most gardens. It was first brought from North America, and has spread all over England. You will easily know it, because its leaves are very like those of the currant-bushes in the kitchen garden, and its pretty hanging clusters of red or pink flowers are shaped like the little green blossoms of our currants and gooseberries. Then in the autumn it has hanging bunches of dark berries, which are not good to eat. A piece of Ribes cut off and stuck in the ground will grow without any trouble.

THE WILD BARBERRY

Another very pretty bush flowers in early summer. This is the Barberry, whose small scarlet fruits used at one time to be put inside sugar plums. The barberry is an interesting shrub, for it has turned some of its leaves into thorns, so that at each joint there is a three-pronged thorn, as well as the smooth, fringed leaves. The wild barberry has yellow flowers with bright red anthers, but there is a garden kind with ever-green leaves, which has deep orange-coloured flowers. They are small and hang in a long spray, and if you are clever you can try an experiment with either the wild or garden barberry.

Look carefully at one of the flowers and you will see that the six stamens are spread out, one lying down upon each petal. At the bottom of the petal, near the middle of the flower, are two bags, out of which oozes honey in drops. The sticky stigma on the top of the seed-box stands up in the middle of the flower.

Now take a needle and touch one of the stamens at its base, just where the honey drops are. It will jump up, as if moved by a spring, and touch the sticky stigma, then after a little while it will fall down again. Now when a bee puts her head in for honey she irritates the stamen so that it jumps up and hits her and she carries the pollen-dust to another flower. Or the anther leaves some pollen on its own stigma, before it falls down again.

But we must go on, for when the "March winds and April showers bring forth May flowers" there will be plenty of shrubs to look at. There is the Spanish Broom, with its bright yellow blossoms shaped like a pea-flower. You can find wild broom growing on the heaths. It is very like gorse, only it has smooth, green stems, and no prickles. But in the wild broom the blossoms grow singly on the stem, while in Spanish broom they form bright yellow clusters. The broom has no honey, but the bees come to it for pollen-dust to make bee-bread.

TREES AND SHRUBS

If there is a Lilac bush growing near the broom you will notice how lovely the two colours, yellow and lilac, look together. You can make a very pretty nosegay from the two shrubs. But you will make a more graceful one, if you can find a Laburnum with its long sprays of golden blossom. The laburnum has plenty of honey in its flowers, and, as the bees have to gnaw a lump to get at it, they often stop a long time at each flower, and you may see many on one tree. Laburnum pods are like small pea-pods, but take care not to eat the seeds in them, for they are very poisonous.

Next the Rhododendrons will be opening their beautiful bunches of red-purple flowers among their glossy, green leaves. These come from North America. But the Elderbush, which grows in the corner, making a pleasant shade over a little seat, is a true English shrub, which almost deserves to be called a tree. It does not bloom much before July, but it is one of the first trees to put out its leaves in the early spring. Though it is not tall, it has very thick stems, and its bark is rough and corky.

You must take the young branches if you want to make pop-guns, for in the old ones the pith is crushed up into quite a tiny space by the rings of wood outside. The leaves of the elder grow opposite to each other on the stem, and each leaf is cut into seven or nine leaflets, with one at the end. The small white flowers grow in very large flat clusters, and leave the sweet elder-berries behind them in the autumn.

RED FLOWER, JAPAN PEAR
WHITE FLOWER, SNOWBALL TREE

TREES AND SHRUBS

If you have not an elder tree in the garden, you will very likely have a Snowball tree (*see* p. 59). This is a garden kind of Guelder rose. Its blossoms are not in a flat bunch as they are on the wild tree. They grow in a ball and they have no stamens or seedbox in them, so they make no seeds. But the leaves turn purple in the autumn and are very lovely.

By this time the big purple Clematis will be out over the porch. It will last in bloom till October, and behind it on the wall grows the Myrtle, which will be covered with white flowers in August. We all know the myrtle so well that it is difficult to believe that it is not a British shrub. It came from the south of France, and now grows in all warm parts of England, keeping our walls green all the year round. Its oval leaves give a delightful scent from the little pockets of oil, which you may see if you look through the leaf at the light.

Bring flowers and leaves of any of the shrubs mentioned.

CHAPTER XI

THE ASH AND THE ELM

NEXT to the oak, the two hardwood trees which are most useful are the ash and the elm. Both these trees grow in the hedgerows as well as in the open fields, and they both blossom quite early in the year, before they put forth their leaves.

You may know Ash stems anywhere, even in winter, by two things. First by the tips of its branches, which are flat, as if they had been pressed under a weight. And secondly by its black buds shaped like little pyramids (*see* p. 63). No other tree has black buds like these. The trunk is an ash-grey colour, and the branches grow very gracefully, first dipping down from the boughs and then tilting up again like the horns of a deer.

In April the ash-buds on the side branches near to the tip begin to open out into clusters of purple-black flowers (2). Each flower is very small. It has no flower-leaves, nothing but a seed-box and two purple stamens. But these tiny flowers are so closely crowded that the whole tree is coloured by them.

TREES AND SHRUBS

Then, at the end of May, the leaf-buds begin to open. The leaves grow opposite to each other on the branches, and each leaf (1) is cut into seven or more leaflets, with an odd one at the end. Many leaves are cut up like this, and you might think each leaflet was a leaf. But if they were leaves, a bud would grow at the base of each, near the stem, and there would be a growing tip at the end. So when there are neither of these you may know that all the leaflets make up one leaf; and when it fades, the whole falls off together.

All through the summer the tree is very beautiful, and its bluish-grey leaves differ from those of any other tree. But early in the autumn they turn yellow and fall. Then you will know the tree by its curious long, flat, narrow fruits (3), which hang in groups from the branches like bunches of keys. In fact, they are called "keys." They hang on sometimes quite into the winter, till the rough winds tear them off.

You may often find a young ash-tree growing in your garden, for they are very hardy. But rabbits are fond of eating the young seedlings, so they have not much chance to grow. Young ash stems are often used for walking-sticks and hop-poles, and the wood, when full-grown, sells very well for coach-building and for making furniture.

We all know Elm-trees so well that perhaps you may think that there is nothing interesting to learn about them. But I wonder if you have noticed that the twigs of an elm grow on the trunk almost to the bottom of the tree unless they are lopped off. And I am almost sure that many of you do not know that the twigs are often covered with little lumps of cork, making the branch look as if it were diseased.

TIP OF A BRANCH OF ASH
1. Leaf of nine Leaflets
2. Flowers
3. Fruit called "keys"

It is really quite healthy, but it tells a secret, namely, that the elm has a very corky bark. Even on the trunk the cork is thick and rugged, and on the small branches it has no room to spread, and has to lie in lumps. The inner part of the bark called the "liber" is very tough, and is used for making mats and ropes.

The common elm, which so often grows in rows between the fields, or is planted on the village green, was brought to England by the Romans. It is not quite at home even now, for its seeds do not ripen, except in very hot summers, and new trees have to be planted from suckers.

TWIG OF ELM-TREE COVERED WITH CORK

The real old elm of England is the Wych elm or Scotch elm. It has not such a tall trunk as the common elm, for its big branches grow out much lower down. Its leaves are bigger, and its seeds ripen and grow, when they are sown. But it is not very common in our country and grows chiefly in Scotland, Wales, and the West of England.

Even in winter you can count a great number of buds on the elm, and when April comes, if you look up through the boughs, you will see a purple tinge all over the top of the tree. This is caused by the tiny purple flowers which burst out on the twigs. Now watch the tree. At the end of April the fresh green leaves peep out of the leaf-buds. But already the seed-boxes are beginning to fall and are blown into heaps by the wind.

ELM TREE TWIGS
1. Twig with Flowers   2. Twig with Ovaries

I am sure you must know these little, flat, green plates, with a lump in the middle where the seed lies. They are blown along the fields, and often down the village street, filling the gutters. If they fall from the Common elm it is very doubtful whether they will grow. But if you have a Wych elm on the green, you may know its seed-boxes, because the seed always lies quite in the middle of the plate, while in the common elm it lies nearer the point. These seeds are ripe and worth sowing.

There are a great many kinds of elm in England, very like each other, but it is easy to know the Cornish elm because it grows such a great deal of cork on its twigs. All the big forest elms are very useful for timber. They sometimes live for four or five hundred years, but the best time for cutting them down is when they are about one hundred and twenty years old.

A great many insects feed on the elm. The most destructive one is a beetle which eats its way down to the inner bark, and sucks the sap. Then the mother beetle works her way down about two inches and makes little galleries all along the tube on each side. In each gallery she lays an egg, and the grubs when they are hatched eat the wood. The trees of whole forests have been killed by this "elm-destroying beetle."

Bring an ash branch to look at the twigs and buds. Find a bunch of ash-keys. Find the corky twigs of the elm, and the green seed-plates in May. Look in decayed elms for the galleries of the elm-destroying beetle.

CHAPTER XII

IN THE PARK

In our great parks you will find the largest and grandest English trees, besides many which are interesting because they come from abroad. Avenues, of a mile or two miles long, are often planted with one kind of tree, chestnut, beech, oak, horse-chestnut, or lime, while in the open ground the oaks and horse-chestnuts grow into much finer trees than in the fields.

We have not yet spoken of the Lime-tree, but you know it quite well, with its straight, smooth trunk, its bright, heart-shaped green leaves, bigger on one side than the other, and pointed at the tip, and its bunches of yellowish green flowers, which grow on a long stalk coming out of the middle of a yellow-green leaf (2, p. 68).

Get some of these flowers in July, or some of the round, downy fruit with ribs on it in the autumn when it is ripe. The leaf out of which they grow is called a *bract*, and is the same kind of leaf as the scales on which the willow stamens, and the pine seeds grow. But in the Lime it has become a long leaf which can be carried by

(ABOVE) ARBUTUS, OR STRAWBERRY TREE IN FLOWER
AND FRUIT
(BELOW) LIME TREE IN FLOWER

the wind. The inner bark or "liber" of the lime tree is very useful in making ropes, and of all trees the bees love this one, for the flowers have a sweet scent and plenty of honey in their cups.

There is another tree, which is almost as useful to the bees, which blooms rather earlier than the lime. This is the Sycamore, whose clusters of green flowers hang from the twigs in May, before the leaves are quite out. The sycamore is a very handsome tree with large leaves cut into five broad divisions. It is really a kind of maple, very like the common English field maple which grows in the hedges. If you stand under a sycamore in warm weather you will often notice that drops fall from it, and you will find that its leaves are sticky. This is because all maples have a great deal of very sugary juice or sap in them, which rises up and oozes out of the leaves, either from cracks made by the leaf being dry, or because some insect has bitten a hole. You must have seen the little green blight-insects which cling on rose trees and other plants, and suck out their juice. Hundreds and thousands of these, besides other bugs (such as the cuckoo-spit, which you find covered with froth), suck the sap of trees. So through the cracks they have made the sugary juice of the sycamore or the maple oozes out over the leaves.

The fruit of these trees is very curious. It is winged like the keys of the ash, but two fruits grow together, so that the two wings spread out like those of a moth *(see*

TREES AND SHRUBS

p. 71). The wings of the Field Maple fruit are spread more widely than those of the sycamore.

Maple wood is very useful for furniture. A great many of our desks and wardrobes are made from American maple. Maple sugar, which American children love, comes from the sugary sap of an American species.

Another tree which you will find in the park is the Walnut, which was brought to England by the Romans. It is a large, spreading tree with a rough trunk and strong, crooked branches. Its leaves are cut like those of the ash, but they are much larger. They have a pretty red tinge when they are young, and always have a strong smell when they are crushed.

These trees grow so quickly that they are twenty feet high in ten years, and then begin to flower and make fruit. They go on growing till they are about seventy feet high. You can see the long catkins hanging from the tree in April just as the leaves are opening. The stamen catkins are at the tip of last year's twigs. But the little group of flowers which will grow into walnuts are on the new twigs, which have just come from buds. In autumn every boy knows the walnut fruit shut up in the green husk, which stains your fingers brown as you peel it off. When the husk is off you can slip a knife between the halves of the hard shell and split them apart. In doing this you divide the two seed-leaves of the seed, which are the parts you eat; and if you look carefully you will

IN THE PARK

see the little white bud and root, lying between them, at the pointed end of the walnut. Walnut wood is very useful for furniture, for it becomes a deep brown when the tree is old, and has very beautiful veins in it.

There is one more tree or shrub which grows only in parks and shrubberies, about which I must tell you, because it is so pretty. But I am not sure you will be able to find one. It is the Arbutus, or Strawberry tree (plate, p. 68) so called because its fruits look like strawberries. It is an evergreen shrub with green, glossy leaves shaped like a bay leaf and very notched at the edge. Its flowers are bell-shaped and waxy like the flowers of the heath, and they hang on bent stalks. But the curious thing about them is, that the fruits take a year to ripen. First they are a pale yellow, then they grow deeper and deeper in colour till they are a bright scarlet, hanging in twos and threes among the dark-green leaves, just when the tree blooms afresh with its pretty, greenish-white flowers.

SYCAMORE TWIG WITH ITS FRUIT

Other trees which you may find in the park are

TREES AND SHRUBS

the Chili pine, or monkey-puzzle, a tree which bears cones and has such prickly leaves close together, that it would indeed puzzle a monkey to climb it, and the large magnolias and tulip-trees which have such beautiful white and pinkish flowers as large as bowls. But these are foreigners and we must be content with knowing about English-growing trees.

Find the flowers and fruit of the lime tree; the leaves of the sycamore sticky with honey-dew; the winged seeds of the maple and the sycamore; the leaves and catkins of the walnut tree. Open a walnut and find the young shoot inside.

CHAPTER XIII

LEAVES—THEIR SHAPE AND POSITION

In the summer when the trees are in full leaf, and you have learnt to know them, you should bring in leafy twigs from each tree and note how the leaves grow on the stem, and what shapes they have.

We have already noticed that some trees, such as the horse-chestnut and the maple, have their leaves opposite to each other on the stem, two growing on each joint, while others, such as the elm and the beech for example, have their leaves alternate, one only growing from each joint. But there are many kinds of alternate leaves, and you will enjoy finding them out.

In the elm and the beech *every other* leaf comes exactly above the one below. Leaf 1 comes on one side of the stem, leaf 2 on the other side, leaf 3 exactly above leaf 1. But if you take a twig of the trembling poplar, or Aspen, it will be leaf 4 which comes above leaf 1. They have crept more slowly round the stem. Then take a twig of oak. You will find that you will have to count six leaves before you find one exactly over the first one.

All these differences have their use, and when you are in the lanes, if you look at the trees, you will see how these arrangements bring the leaves into positions where they can best get light and air.

The next thing to look at is the shape of the leaves themselves. Botanists have a great many names to describe the shapes, the edges, the veins, and the divisions of leaves. I can only tell you of a few, so that you may keep your eyes open and notice others.

Leaves which are whole, so that you cannot pull off one piece without tearing it away from the rest, are called *simple*. The leaves of the elm, beech, sweet-chestnut, lime, oak, willow, sycamore, and many others are *simple*.

Leaves which are cut into separate leaflets, so that you can pull one off without touching the others, are called *compound*. The leaves of the horse-chestnut, ash, rose, rowan-tree, and elder are *compound*. You will remember that you know the divisions are leaflets and not leaves, because there is no growing tip at the end, and there are no buds in the angles. The leaflets grow out from the top of the leaf stalk (horse-chestnut), or from the narrow, green line, up the middle (rose), which is not a stalk, but the midrib of the leaf.

Now take all the simple leaves you have, and see what shapes they are. The best way to find out this is to lay a leaf on your slate and draw a line round it. This is very easy with a beech leaf, or the leaf of a sweet-chestnut. But when you take an oak leaf, you will want to know whether you are to run in and out of the divisions.

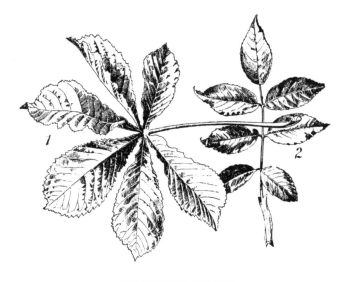

COMPOUND LEAVES
1. Horse Chestnut   2. Rose

For the *shape* of a leaf you are not to do this. You are to begin at the leaf stalk and run round the *outside* points of the leaf all the way till you come back to the leaf stalk again. If you go round a maple leaf like this you will have a shape something like a *kidney*. A sycamore leaf will be more *heart-shaped*, longer, and ending in a blunt tip. An oak leaf will be *oblong*, longer than it is broad. The leaf of an elm or a beech you will find is shaped like an *egg*, and so is called *oval*, while the leaf of the sweet-chestnut is narrow and long. Lastly, if you take a lime leaf it will be heart-shaped, but uneven, one side of the leaf larger than the other. It is called *oblique*.

Now let us see how much the different leaves are cut. Some, like those of the lilac and ivy, are smooth at the edge. Others are *wavy*, and the holly has prickles at the end of its waves to protect it. But, if you look at holly leaves near the top of a tree where the cattle cannot reach, you will often find they do not take the trouble to grow prickles.

Other leaves have *teeth* round the edge. The leaf of the sweet-chestnut is toothed like a *saw*. So is a birch leaf, but if you look closely you will find it has two sets of teeth. The large teeth have their edges cut into small teeth. This leaf has a *double-sawed* edge. Some leaves again are very deeply cut into divisions or lobes. An oak leaf is cut, sometimes only in a wavy line, and sometimes into quite large divisions. A sycamore leaf has five large pointed divisions or *lobes*.

Get these two leaves and compare them. You will see that the veins which make the skeleton of the different shapes are not the same. In the sycamore leaf the large veins, or ribs, start from the top of the stalk, and spread out like five fingers, while the little veins start out from them. A leaf like this is called a palm-veined or *palmate-veined* leaf because the veins are like fingers on a hand. In the oak leaf, on the contrary, one long rib runs up the middle. The smaller ones start

LEAVES—THEIR SHAPE AND POSITION

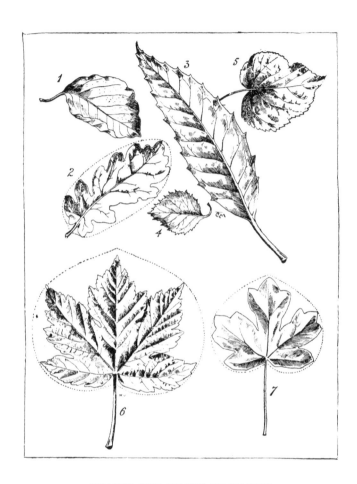

SHAPES AND EDGES OF LEAVES

1. BEECH—*oval, edge wavy*
2. OAK—*oblong, deeply wavy*
3. SWEET CHESTNUT—*narrow, broadly sawed*
4. BIRCH—*doubly sawed*
5. LIME—*heart-shaped and oblique*
6. SYCAMORE—*heart-shaped, five-lobed*
7. MAPLE—*kidney-shaped, five-lobed*

from it, like the featherlets of a bird's feather. So an oak leaf is said to be feather-veined or *pinnate-veined*, from *pinna*, a feather.

Now take the *compound* leaves of the horse-chestnut, ash, and rose. In the horse-chestnut the *leaflets* grow just like the *veins* of the sycamore. Seven fingers start from the top of the leaf stalk and spread out like fingers, so it is called a *palmate* leaf. But the ash and the rose have a rib up the middle and the separate leaflets are arranged feather-wise. So these leaves are called *pinnate*.

There are a great many leaves with shapes between these, and if you collect them and arrange them in an old copy book, you will soon get an idea of the meaning of their names.

Describe the leaves of the oak, horse-chestnut, and elm and their position on the stem. Arrange any simple leaves and compound leaves you can find in a copy book and describe them.

CPSIA information can be obtained
at www.ICGtesting.com
Printed in the USA
BVHW020520210620
581956BV00001B/18